Volcanoes

Volcanoes

Trudi Strain Trueit

Watts LIBRARY™

Franklin Watts
A Division of Scholastic Inc.
New York • Toronto • London • Auckland • Sydney
Mexico City • New Delhi • Hong Kong
Danbury, Connecticut

*For Robin and everyone who lost a loved one
on Mount St. Helens, May 18, 1980.*

Note to readers: Definitions for words in **bold** can be found in the Glossary at the back of this book.

Photographs ©: 2003: AP/Wide World Photos: 5 right, 6 (Jack Smith), 14 (Roger Werth); Bruce Coleman Inc.: 2, 5, 29 (Phil Degginger), 24, 39 (Nicholas deVore III), 15 (Fritz Polking/POLKI), 31 (W. Stoy); Corbis Images: 38 (Robert Holmes), cover (Jim Sugar Photography), 36; Dr. David Johnston: 9; Francine Coloma: 40, 43, 45 bottom, 45 top, 47; Photo Researchers, NY: 16, 17 (Stephanie Dinkins), 19 (David Hardy/SPL), 23 (Mikkel Juul Jensen/Bonnier Publications/SPL), 34 (Leonard Lee Rue III), 12 (David Weintraub); Visuals Unlimited/A.J. Copley: 26.

Illustration on page 22 by Bernard Adnet

The photograph on the cover shows the eruption of the Puu Oo cone of the Hawaiian volcano of Kilauea. The photograph opposite the title page shows the eruption of Mauna Loa, also in Hawaii.

Library of Congress Cataloging-in-Publication Data

Trueit, Trudi Strain.
    Volcanoes / Trudi Strain Trueit.
        p. cm. — (Watts library)
    Summary: Discusses the formation and characteristics of volcanoes, the causes and effects of their eruption, and describes specific volcanic eruptions such as that of Mount St. Helens in 1980. Includes bibliographical references and index.
    ISBN 0-531-12198-4 (lib. bdg.)   0-531-16244-3 (pbk.)
    1. Volcanoes—Juvenile literature. [1. Volcanoes.] I. Title. II. Series.
QE521.3 .T785 2003
551.21—dc21   2002011647

Contents

For many Americans, the eruption of Mount St. Helens in May 1980 was their most direct experience of the destructive power of a volcano.

Chapter One

Black Sunday

In the 1970s, Mount St. Helens was one of the most climbed peaks in the Cascade Mountain Range. Each year, thousands of people flocked to southwestern Washington state to hike the 9,677-foot (2,950-meter) mountain and enjoy the breathtaking, peaceful view. The volcano was so striking that photographers from around the world came to snap pictures of the perfectly shaped pyramid for postcards and calendars. But on May 18, 1980, the still beauty of Mount St. Helens was shattered. That was the morning the sleeping giant awoke.

Two months earlier, a series of small earthquakes signaled that the mountain was beginning to stir. The youngest volcano in the Cascades, Mount St. Helens had erupted about once each century throughout recorded history, the last time in 1857. Because of this, it was considered an active volcano. Volcanoes are classified as active, dormant, or extinct. **Active volcanoes** are either currently erupting or have erupted at least once in the last ten thousand years. These types of volcanoes are expected to erupt again. **Dormant volcanoes** have not erupted in the last 10,000 years but may erupt in the future. They are "sleeping" and no one can predict when or if they will awaken. **Extinct volcanoes** appear to have finished their life cycle and are not expected to erupt anymore (although sometimes they do).

On March 27, 1980, a burst of steam and **ash**, tiny bits of volcanic rock, tore through the summit of Mount St. Helens. By late spring, more than ten thousand earthquakes had trembled within the volcano; all were centered beneath a bulge that had appeared on the north side. The United States Geological Survey (USGS), a government agency that keeps tabs on the forces of nature, monitored the volcano around the clock. **Geologists**, scientists who study the origin and structure of Earth, determined the growing bulge meant a mixture of melted rock and gases, called **magma**, was rising inside the cone—a sure sign that the volcano was getting ready to erupt. But when?

Volcano Country

Nearly 10 percent of Earth's 1,500 active volcanoes are located in the United States—in Alaska, Hawaii, Washington, Oregon, and California.

This Is It!

At dawn on Sunday, May 18, volcanologist Dr. David Johnston was on duty at Coldwater 2 Observation Post, 6 miles (10 kilometers) north of the summit. A **volcanologist** is a geologist who specializes in studying and monitoring volcanoes. Inside the 20-foot (6-m) trailer, Johnston saw little change in the instruments measuring ground movement,

Volcanologist David Johnston calmly takes notes at Coldwater II Observation Post on May 17, 1980, just a day before Mount St. Helens was to erupt with such unprecedented force.

A Tragic Toll

Considered the most destructive volcanic eruption ever to occur in the continental United States, the Mount St. Helens explosion

- destroyed enough trees to build 300,000 homes.
- killed 12 million salmon, 11,000 rabbits, 5,000 deer, 1,500 elk, and 14 out of 32 species of small animals.
- created 3.7 billion cubic yards of mud, ash, and rock; enough debris to bury downtown Seattle to the tip of the Space Needle.
- pumped out 540 million tons of ash. Imagine a football field piled 150 miles (240 km) high with ash.
- caused more than $1 billion in damages.

volcanic gas emissions, and the size of the bulge, which was now a mile (1.6 km) wide. He radioed the main observatory in Vancouver, 50 miles (80 km) away, that all was quiet.

At 8:32 A.M., a 5.1 magnitude earthquake shook the volcano. Seconds later the bulge broke loose, triggering one of the largest landslides in history. The **avalanche** of snow, rock, mud, and debris charged into the valleys below at more than 180 miles (290 km) per hour. Exposed to open air, the gases in magma, mainly sulfur dioxide and carbon dioxide, explode like a shaken can of soda (in fact, tiny amounts of carbon dioxide are used to put the fizz in soft drinks). When the rock covering the magma on Mount St. Helens gave way that is exactly what happened. At 8:39 A.M., an eruption blew sideways out of the north face of the mountain at speeds up to 600 miles (965 km) per hour. In seconds, the top 1,300 feet (400 m) of Mount St. Helens had blown away completely.

Johnston's two-way radio crackled. "Vancouver! Vancouver!" he shouted. "This is it!"

The force of the eruption vaporized trees, plants, animals—everything within 8 miles (13 km) of the blast. Reaching temperatures of more than 660° F (350° C), the hot gases and rock that spewed from the crater melted more than 70 percent of the ice and snow on the mountain. The water mixed with rocks, trees, and soil to form powerful mudflows called **lahars**. Fiercely hot waves of gas, ash, and rock, called **pyroclastic flows**, poured out of the mountain and swept through the valleys below. In nearby Spirit Lake and Toutle River, temperatures topped 100° F (38° C). Witnesses reported seeing fish trying to leap out of the scalding water.

Fifty-seven people were unable to escape the volcano's fury. Most died from inhaling the hot, poisonous ash that enveloped them. Some were buried under the torrential lahars and pyroclastic flows, while others were burned alive. A few of the dead were found still holding their cameras. Twenty-seven people were never found. Coldwater 2 Observatory was directly in the path of the eruption. By the time rescuers arrived, the area was buried under tons of mud and ash. There was no sign of Dr. Johnston or the trailer. Two hundred people trapped on the mountain did survive, thanks mainly to National Guard helicopters that airlifted them to safety.

The eruption produced an **ash cloud** that took less than 20 minutes to rise 15 miles (24 km) into the sky. Prevailing winds

A second major eruption of Mount St. Helens occurred on July 22, 1980, a little more than two months after the first.

blew the plume over eastern Washington. In Spokane, 250 miles (400 km) away, day turned to night as 7 inches (18 centimeters) of ash fell like gray snowflakes. In three days, ash from St. Helens had dusted cities from Idaho to the East Coast. In two weeks, the ash cloud circled the globe. Some of the tiniest **dust** particles remained in the upper atmosphere for years afterward.

Out of the Ashes

Immediately after the explosion, it seemed as if nothing within a 10-mile (16-km) radius of the mountain possibly could have survived. Only charred rocks and steaming stumps dotted the gray, muddy moonscape. Mile after mile of forest had been blown down in crisscross patterns, trees flattened against the hillsides as if they were matchsticks.

Yet even after such massive devastation, there were signs of life. Ants, beetles, pocket gophers, mice, and other burrowing animals had survived. On the edges of the blast zone, Pacific silver firs and mountain hemlocks were alive. Within days of the eruption, desert birds such as meadowlarks and rock wrens returned to the area. Native mountain bluebirds, ravens, and robins soon followed.

A few months later, magma in the crater of St. Helens began rising to form a lava dome, a normal occurrence in a volcano of this kind. By 1986, the dome had grown nearly 900 feet (275 m) above the crater floor. Mount St. Helens belched steam and ash until the fall of 1986, when she stopped erupt-

This is Mount St. Helens as it appears today from the viewing deck outside the Johnston Ridge Observatory, which is about five miles away. The observatory is the closest the public can come to the volcano by car.

ing altogether. Minor earthquakes continued through the late 1990s.

Over time, deer, elk, and other wildlife populations in the region rebounded. Beneath the ash, the hearty roots of plants such as fireweed, pearly everlasting, and Canada thistle sent up new sprouts. Winds scattered the seeds of lupines, red alder, and evergreen trees across the blast zone. Nearly ten million trees were planted to form fourteen thousand acres of forest.

Dangerous Beauty

At 14,410 feet (4,392 m), Mount Rainier is the tallest peak in the Cascades and one of the most dangerous in the world, according to scientists. Its 35 miles (56 km) of glaciers contain five times as much snow as all the other volcanoes in the chain combined. Scientists fear the intense heat of a volcanic blast would cause a rapid snowmelt, sending massive lahars into the heavily populated valleys below.

Today, more than three million people visit the Mount St. Helens National Volcanic Monument each year. They stand atop the Johnston Ridge Observatory, named in memory of David Johnston and located near where he died. Mount St. Helens is now quiet, but volcanologists continue to study, watch, and wait. They know the sleeping giant will one day awaken again, and it will probably happen before the end of this century.

Vulcano, an island in the Italian chain known as the Aeolians, was named for the Roman god Vulcan. The word volcano comes from the same source.

Chapter Two

Volcano Birth

Did you know that if it weren't for volcanoes, we might not be here? Billions of years ago, millions of volcanic eruptions around the globe released tons of gases, lava, and rock. The gases created the atmosphere and the air we breathe. The venting steam, which was water in the form of gas, produced clouds and rain. The falling raindrops filled the oceans and seas with precious water. The hot lava cooled to become part of Earth's crust, shaping valleys, mountains, and islands. Volcanoes above and below sea level formed more than 80 percent of the planet's surface.

A **volcano** is any opening, or **vent**, in the surface of Earth where materials such as gases, magma, and/or rock emerge. It may be a snowy, steep-sloped mountain, a jumble of holes across a flat plain, or a long crack, called a **fissure**, in the ocean floor. Today, about sixty volcanoes on land erupt each year, while thousands more explode beneath the oceans. Volcanoes are vital to our survival, recycling the life-giving gases and rock that keep our world in balance.

Planet of Fire

Although it might not appear very hot on the surface, deep beneath your feet, Earth is a fiery planet. Volcanoes are cooling vents that allow some of the heat that is brewing within the globe to escape. About 3,900 miles (6,300 km) beneath the ground lay the center, or **core**, of Earth. Made primarily of nickel and iron, the core has two layers: the outer core and the inner core. Scientists estimate that the liquid outer core is almost as hot as the surface of the Sun, about 9,000° F (5,000° C), while the solid inner core likely tops 12,000° F (6,600° C). Surrounding the core is the **mantle**, a layer of heat-softened rock. Making up more than 70 percent of the planet, the mantle extends from about 30 miles (50 km) to 1,800 miles (2,900 km) below the surface. Temperatures of up to 7,500° F (4,150° C) in the mantle keep the heat-softened rock flowing slowly in large currents.

Above the mantle sits Earth's **crust**, a rocky outer covering that makes up just 1 percent of the entire planet. The

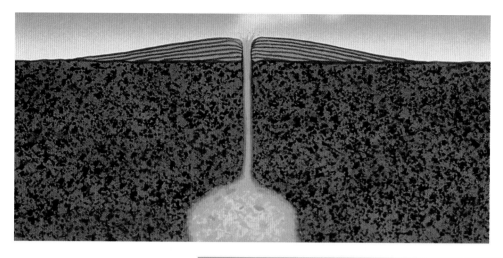

This diagram represents the evolution of a volcano. At left, the volcano is in its earliest stages, when occasional eruptions create only a shallow crater.

As the volcano ages, the crater becomes larger and the magma beneath moves upward (right). Finally, the crater collapses into the magma, often because of landslides. The result is a catastrophic eruption (below), like the one of Mount St. Helens in 1980.

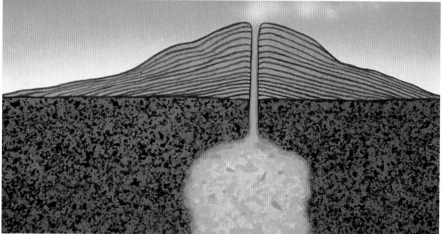

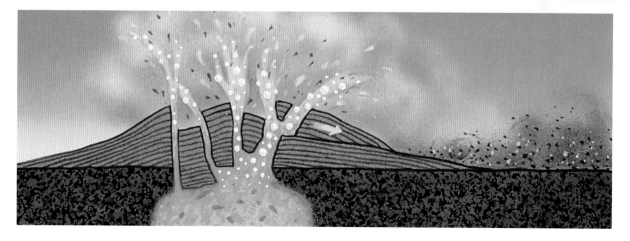

Tapping Into Nature

Many countries, including the Philippines, New Zealand, Italy, and the United States, drill into Earth's crust to harness **geothermal energy**, tapping wells of steam and hot water that are used to produce electricity. The biggest drawback to using geothermal energy is that it takes a lot of heat to create a small amount of power. Iceland, an island that sits over a hot spot atop the Mid-Atlantic Ridge, has had the most success harnessing the planet's heat. With about twenty-five active volcanoes and numerous thermal hot springs, boiling mud lakes, and geysers, this arctic nation relies on geothermal energy to power most of its capital, Reykjavik, a city of approximately 150,000 people.

crust is broken up into many pieces, much like a cracked eggshell. There are eight large sections, or **tectonic plates**, and many smaller ones. The plates may carry continents, islands, oceans, or any combination of the three. Oceanic crust is about 3 to 6 miles (5 to 10 km) thick, while continental crust is about 25 to 55 miles (40 to 90 km) thick. Fueled by the currents of the partially melted materials from the mantle, tectonic plates travel at the slow rate of 0.5 to 3 inches (2 to 8 cm) per year. As they move, plates may bump, separate, or slip past one another.

Mountains are created when continental crust collides and buckles, crumpling upward. For volcanoes to form, a key ingredient must be present: magma. In some places on Earth, hot rock moves upward from the mantle into the crust. As it squeezes between the heavier, solid rock surrounding it, the hot rock melts into magma. Liquid magma collects in large pools a few miles (kilometers) below the surface that feed **magma chambers**. At the top of the chambers, **feeder pipes** carry the magma on its upward journey. As magma rises, decreasing pressure causes it to get hotter. The drop in pressure also causes gases within the magma to expand (remember that shaken can of soda pop?). Pressure and gases propel magma upward through one or more openings in the crust, creating a volcanic eruption. Magma that flows onto the surface of the planet is known as **lava**.

Unique Peaks

Because volcanoes form under specific conditions, they can only be found in certain places on Earth: **rift zones, subduction zones**, and **hot spots**. A rift zone is an area where tectonic plates are slowly spreading apart. This separation allows hot magma to bubble up between deep, narrow vents called fissures. Undersea eruptions may form a chain of volcanoes along **oceanic ridges**. Oceanic ridges circle Earth's ocean floors like seams on a baseball. The Mid-Atlantic Ridge is a string of rift volcanoes that stretches from the Arctic Circle to the southern Atlantic Ocean and around the globe to the Pacific Ocean. As new crust is being formed in rift zones, old crust is being pushed back into the mantle at subduction zones. When two tectonic plates collide and one slides under the other, the area of the collision is called a subduction zone. Oceanic plates are denser than continental plates, so they sink downward at the point where the two plates meet, forming a

The area outlined with small triangles is called the Ring of Fire by scientists. It is a region of intense seismic and volcanic activity.

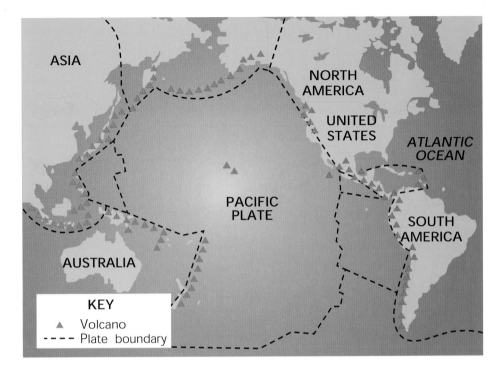

ASIA

NORTH AMERICA

UNITED STATES

ATLANTIC OCEAN

PACIFIC PLATE

SOUTH AMERICA

AUSTRALIA

KEY
▲ Volcano
--- Plate boundary

Islands of Inferno

With nearly 130 active volcanoes strung out across 13,700 islands, Indonesia is one of the most volcanic regions on Earth.

trench on the ocean floor. As the oceanic plate descends, some of it melts. The recycled magma rises upward through the cracks in the crust near the rim of the continental plate to form volcanoes. Mount St. Helens and the Cascade chain were formed by the Cascadia Subduction Zone. This is where the 1,000-mile (1,600-km) long Juan de Fuca oceanic plate is being subducted under the North American Plate.

Nearly half of the planet's active volcanoes bubble, burp, and blast in subduction zones surrounding the Pacific Ocean. Since the region is such a hotbed of volcanic and earthquake activity, it is called the **Ring of Fire**. In the western Pacific, the Ring of Fire includes Mount Fuji in Japan, Mount Pinatubo in the Philippines, and Mount Tambora in Indonesia. On the eastern side of the Pacific sit the Andes in South America, the Cascades, and Alaska's Aleutian Islands.

A hot spot is an area where a rising column of magma is pushing upward through the crust to form a volcano. It may occur anywhere on a plate. While tectonic plates are

This computer illustration shows the process by which the Hawaiian islands were formed from undersea volcanic eruptions.

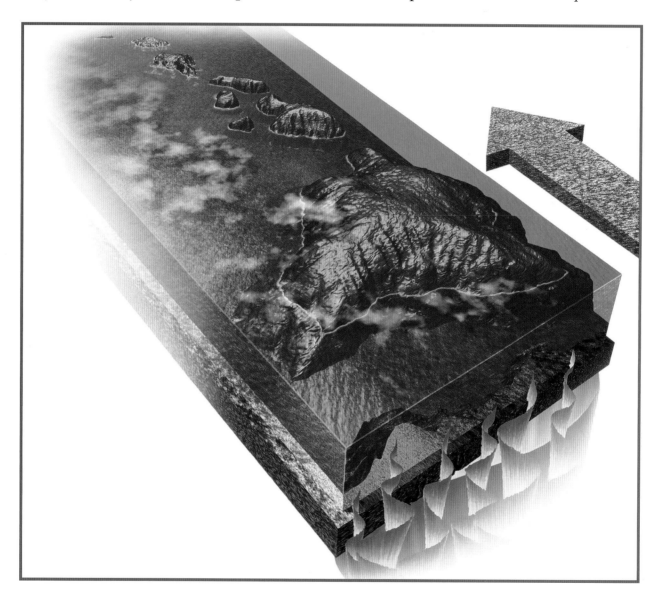

Clouds blanket the Hawaiian volcano of Mauna Loa, which is the largest on Earth. Mauna Loa has erupted 33 times since 1843.

constantly on the move, hot spots remain in the same place. For the past 75 million years, a hot spot beneath Earth's crust has been forming the Hawaiian Islands. As the Pacific Plate passes over it, a single volcano, or a **seamount**, comes to life. When a seamount rises out of the water, it becomes an island. Over time, the plate moves the island away from the hot spot, the aging volcano goes extinct, and a new seamount is born. The oldest volcanoes in the northwestern segment of the Hawaiian Islands, such as Niiahu, died out millions of years ago. But the youngest island, the Big Island of Hawaii, is still growing, fueled by magma rising up through the Pacific Plate. Mauna Loa on the Big Island is the largest active volcano in the world. Its base rises 30,000 feet (9,140 m) from the seafloor, yet only the top 13,680 feet (4,170 m) are visible above the water. The seamount Loihi is the newest undersea volcano being formed over the hot spot. Located 20 miles (32 km) off the coast of the Big Island, it is already 9,000 feet (2,750 m) tall. In about fifty thousand years, Loihi will poke its tip above the waves to become the next island in the chain.

These red cinders are an example of pyroclastic material.

Chapter Three

Eruption!

Somewhere in the world, at least one volcano will ooze, splatter, or explode this week. Most volcanic eruptions last from a few days to about six months. The debris that bursts from a volcano is known as **pyroclastic material**. "Pyroclastic" comes from Greek words meaning "fire fragment."

Volcanoes spew their pyroclastic material in falls and flows. In a **pyroclastic fall**, an explosive eruption sends particles of rock and lava, called **tephra**, into the air. Each fragment is named for its size. The smallest tephra is dust, pieces of rock so tiny that they may float into the upper atmosphere. Rocks slightly larger than dust, measuring about 0.08 inches (2 millimeters), are called ash. Ash particles may be small and smooth, resembling powdered sugar, or they may be a bit larger and grittier, like grains of rice. **Cinders** are bigger than ash, but usually measure no more than 2 inches (5 cm) wide. Cinders are sometimes called "lapilli," an Italian word that means "little stones." Any chunks of rock larger than cinders are referred to as **blocks**. Blocks may be the size of a book, a car, or even a house.

Heavy dust and ash falls may take a devastating toll on the environment, destroying crops, killing wildlife, and even affecting the weather. In April of 1815, Indonesia's Mount Tambora exploded with the power of 25,000 1-megaton bombs. The volcano pumped more than 25 cubic miles (40 cubic km) of tephra into the atmosphere. The following summer, unusually cold weather struck parts of North America and Europe, a result of the ash and gases blocking sunlight. In the middle of July, crops shriveled, ponds froze, and snow fell in New England. In much of the northern hemisphere, 1816 would forever be remembered as "the year without a summer."

Sometimes, a volcanic eruption sends out a debris cloud so heavy that it cannot rise into the air. Instead, it acts like a tidal wave on land. Pyroclastic flows of hot gas, lava, and rock may sweep over the surface at speeds of 100 miles (160 km) per hour or more. On May 8, 1902, a violent eruption tore through Mount Pelée on the Caribbean island of Martinique.

A Dash of Ash

Ash is rich in minerals and nutrients and, in amounts less than 8 inches (20 cm), is good for the soil. For centuries, Italian grape-growers have sprinkled ash from Mount Etna on their crops as fertilizer.

Within minutes, pyroclastic flows charged into the valleys below, burying almost the entire town of St. Pierre. There was no warning and no time to escape. All but two of the town's thirty thousand residents died.

Lava flows are the result of smaller eruptions, often from rift or Hawaiian volcanoes. A lava flow moves much more slowly than a pyroclastic flow, about 5 to 50 miles (8 to 80 km) per hour. But it is still quite dangerous. When Africa's Mount Nyiragongo suddenly erupted in January of 2002, rivers of

Lava flows from Mauna Loa. During Mauna Loa's most recent eruption, in 1984, lava advanced to within four miles of the town of Hilo.

Strange Stuff that Spews

Type	What is it?	Weird facts
Vog (volcanic smog)	Sulfur dioxide gas reacting with sunlight, water, oxygen, and dust in the air.	Hawaii's Kilauea volcano pumps out 2,000 tons of sulfur dioxide everyday, producing a haze of vog pollution clouds. Vog may produce acid rain—a threat to forests, people, crops, wildlife, and water supplies around the world.
Pumice	Volcanic rock filled with gas bubbles.	Pumice cools before its gases have time to escape, creating rock that looks like a sponge and is sometimes light enough to float on water.
Lava bombs	Cinder or block-sized globs of liquid lava.	As they rocket out of a volcano, lava bombs look like red comets. In flight, the cooling lava may whistle as it is twisted into unusual shapes (sometimes resembling footballs).
Pillow lava	Sacklike blobs of cooled lava formed by undersea volcanoes near rift zones or by lava flowing into water	Beneath the ocean, frigid waters quickly cool erupting lava into small mounds of rock. Along the Mid-Atlantic Ridge, stacks of pillow lava sculpt hills more than 100 feet (30 meters) high.
Pele's hair	Erupting lava that is cooled and stretched by the wind to form long, thin fibers of glass.	Many Hawaiians believe Pele, the goddess of volcanoes, lives in Kilauea volcano and, when angry, causes Hawaii's vocanoes to explode. Lava that cools into glass beads is called **Pele's tears**

lava rolled through the streets of downtown Goma, 30 miles (50 km) to the south. The intense heat ignited oil, sparking numerous fires that raced through the city. Sixty people were killed and more than 500,000 were left homeless as they ran for their lives.

There are two types of lava flows, **pahoehoe** and **aa**. Both take their names from the Hawaiian language. Pahoehoe (pronounced *Pah*-hoy-*hoy*) is a runny lava flow that cools to either a smooth or wrinkly surface. Sometimes, after the outer skin has hardened into a black crust, lava continues to move through tunnels beneath it. These currents wrinkle the skin into what looks like twisted rope. Aa (ah-ah) clots as it erupts, creating a stream of liquid lava that contains thick cinders. When it hardens, the rough aa with its jutting cinder chunks may be several hundred feet thick (and hard to walk on). Aa travels forward in surges, tumbling over itself like soil being bulldozed.

Lava cools and hardens in anywhere from a couple of days to a couple of weeks.

Do You Smell Something?

Why do some volcanoes roar to life in a burst of fireworks, while others barely erupt a splash of lava? Magma is the recipe for an eruption. Runny magma allows volcanic gases to escape gradually, producing a smaller eruption. Thicker magma traps gases, which are then released in a far more powerful blast.

Magma gases are made up of water vapor (H_2O), sulfur dioxide (SO_2), carbon dioxide (CO_2), and small amounts of other gases such as hydrogen sulfide (H_2S) and carbon monoxide (CO). Volcanic gases are a hot, toxic brew. Sulfur dioxide burns the eyes, nose, and throat, often causing breathing difficulties. Carbon dioxide has no color or odor, but is deadly. Because it is heavier than air, CO_2 may hug the ground as it moves with the pyroclastic flow, killing wildlife and people without warning. Mammoth Mountain in the Sierra Nevada regularly vents CO_2, occasionally requiring the U.S. Forestry Service to close nearby campgrounds so campers won't suffocate.

I Give It an Eight

In 1982, scientists began ranking past and present volcanic eruptions from 0 to 8 on the **Volcanic Explosivity Index (VEI)**. Several factors are considered when rating each eruption: the force of the explosion, the amount of debris released, the height of ash cloud, the type of eruption, and how long the erruption lasted. Each step on the scale represents a ten-fold increase in volcanic debris. Hawaiian volcanoes, with their smaller fountains of lava, usually measure 0 (non-explosive) or 1 (gentle). Most volcanic eruptions rate less than 2 on the scale. The Mount St. Helens blast in 1980 measured a 5. Eruptions of 5 or higher occur in the world about once every twenty years. Only one volcanic blast has earned a VEI 7 in the last thousand years. The 1815 eruption of Mount Tambora on the Indonesian island of Sumbawa was considered a supercolossal eruption. The gases, lava, and ash fall covered the ground up to a foot (30 cm) deep on Sumbawa and surrounding islands, destroying crops for hundreds of miles (km). About ten thousand people were killed by the flows and deadly gases from the initial blast. Another 82,000 died the following year from starvation because of the extensive crop loss. In recorded history, there have been no VEI 8 eruptions, known as megacolassal eruptions, on Earth.

Earth's Deadliest Eruptions

Volcano	Year	Deaths	Major Cause of Death	VEI Rank
1. Tambora, Indonesia	1815	92,000	Starvation	7, Supercolossal
2. Krakatoa, Indonesia	1883	36,000	Tsunami (huge ocean wave triggered by eruption)	6, Colossal
3. Pelée, Martinique	1902	30,000	Pyroclastic flows	4, Cataclysmic
4. Nevado del Ruiz, Colombia	1985	25,000	Lahars	3, Severe
5. Unzen, Japan	1792	15,000	Volcano collapse, landslides, tsunami	3, Severe

This volcanic cinder cone is on Bartolome, which is one of the Galapagos Islands, a chain, or archipelago, in the Pacific Ocean west of the South American nation of Ecuador.

Chapter Four

The Face of a Volcano

Deep beneath the sea, beds of rock pillars spurt billows of black smoke as if they are chimneys from a lost undersea civilization. On a rugged, barren landscape, a shallow vent blasts out bits of rock, giving rise to a new volcano that will grow several hundred feet in just a few days. Each volcano on Earth is a distinct creation, its shape helping to reveal how it was formed. Based on the type of magma, vent, and style of eruption, scientists group volcanoes into four main

On the morning of November 14, 1963, a cook on a fishing boat off the southern tip of Iceland witnessed a rare and amazing sight. What he thought was black smoke from a ship on fire was actually the birth pains of Surtsey, an island being formed by undersea volcanic eruptions.

categories: **cinder cones**, **stratovolcanoes**, **lava domes**, and **shield volcanoes**.

Cinder cones are formed from thick magma erupting from a single vent. The lava breaks apart in flight, cooling into cinders that fall around the volcano to form a small, circular cone. Because cinders can easily wash away or collapse, this type of volcano rarely reaches more than 1,000 feet (300 m). In February of 1943, a cinder cone volcano began erupting in the mountainous village of Paricutin, west of Mexico City. It grew 33 feet (10 m) in just one day and, in two months, had grown to more than 1,000 feet (300 m). Most cinder cones erupt for a brief time before going extinct, which is what happened in Mexico. Over several years, the eruptions at Paricutin fizzled. On March 4,

Mount Fuji stands majestically over the blue waters of Kawaguchi Lake on the Japanese island of Honshu. Mount Fuji is actually three different volcanoes.

1952, nine years after it first exploded onto the surface of the planet, the 1,732-foot (528-m) volcano went extinct.

Stratovolcanoes, also called composite volcanoes, are the towering, steep-sided cones most people picture when they think of volcanoes. Stratovolcanoes make up more than two-thirds of the active volcanoes that have erupted on land throughout history. Two different types of eruptions go into forming a stratovolcano: a quiet eruption of flowing lava followed by a more explosive eruption of ash and rock. The sequence repeats many times, building the volcano layer by layer to a height of 8,000 feet (2,400 m) or more. Some of the most magnificent volcanoes in the world are stratovolcanoes, including Mount St. Helens, Mount Fuji, and Mount Cotopaxi in Ecuador.

Lava domes are formed when lava oozes from a volcano like toothpaste and, because it is too thick to flow very far, cools and hardens around the vent. Lava domes are often found inside the craters and calderas of stratovolcanoes. Since they usually build from within, lava domes may form unusually shaped

Collapsing Calderas

A **caldera** is formed when the force of one or more eruptions weakens a volcanic cone so that it collapses into its own magma chamber. Scientists figure that nearly seven thousand years ago, a series of powerful blasts caused the cone of Oregon's Mount Mazama to fall, creating a caldera 6 miles (10 km) wide and 2,000 feet (600 m) deep. Over time, rainwater filled the caldera to create Crater Lake, the deepest lake in North America.

Lassen Peak, in California's Cascades mountain range, shimmers above and in the waters of the appropriately named Reflection Lake.

shafts, spines, or knobs above the vent. Lassen Peak in northern California, part of the Cascade Range, is one of the largest lava dome volcanoes in the world. The 3,187-foot (10,457-m) lava dome is a plug that grew from the crater of Mount Broke-off more than 27,000 years ago. Lassen Peak last erupted in 1921 but the area still contains mud pots, hot springs, and **fumaroles**, which are vents that belch gases and steam.

Shield volcanoes have gently sloping cones and wide bases. They are formed by lava pouring or spurting out of one or more vents. The hot, fluid lava may travel a great distance before it cools into a thin, sheetlike layer. Layer after layer of cooled lava slowly builds the shield volcano, which may grow to a diameter of 4 miles (6 km) and a height of 2,000 feet (600 m) or more. This makes them much larger than any other type of volcano. Hawaii's volcanoes, including the active Mauna Loa and Kilauea volcanoes, are shield volcanoes. **Fissure volcanoes** are a type of shield volcano in which lava erupts from a long fissure,

This aerial view provides a look into the Iki crater of Kilauea, a volcano in Hawaii. Volcanologists believe Kilauea may be the most active volcano on Earth.

or crack, on land or under the sea. The lava may flow for thousands of miles, cooling into wide sheets that form **flood basalts**. More than 17 million years ago, three hundred eruptions from fissure volcanoes in eastern Oregon, Washington, and western Idaho created the Columbia Plateau, a 100,000-square mile (59,000 square-km) flood basalt. Today, Iceland is the only place where active fissure volcanoes can be found on land.

Volcanoes of Life

Along oceanic ridges, scientists have discovered volcanic chimneys called **black smokers**. Seawater seeping into cracks in the ocean floor is heated by magma and spewed from the vents of rock columns up to 100 feet (30 m) tall. The billowy, black clouds form when cold ocean water rapidly cools sulfur, copper, and other minerals in the erupting lava. Although the chemicals spouting from black smokers would be toxic to animals in other environments, in the deepest part of the sea they are vital to life. Bacteria feed on the hot chemical stew, and in turn provide food for animals such as giant clams, crabs, and tube worms.

Volcanologist Francine Coloma has studied the Hawaiian volcanoes of Kilauea, Mauna Loa, and Hualalai.

Chapter Five

In the Hot Zone

Volcanologist Francine Coloma steps out of a helicopter onto the steaming, black crust of Hawaii's Kilauea volcano. The hot air is thick with the rotten-egg stench of sulfur. She wears a gas mask to keep from inhaling the toxic fumes. As Coloma's hiking boots crunch over the sharp edges of the lava field, she can see fiery molten lava through the cracks beneath her feet. She is the first person ever to set foot on this freshly formed land, even if it means she can't stay in one

Color Clues

You can tell how hot lava is by its color. At about 2,400° F (1350° C), the hottest lava gets, it is yellowish-white. As it cools, lava turns orange and then red before finally changing to gray or black.

place very long. If she did not keep moving, the soles of her boots would melt.

Being a volcanologist with the USGS Hawaiian Volcano Observatory can be a risky job. But it is also an exciting one. As a child growing up in Hilo, Hawaii, Coloma would sit on her roof at twilight, captivated by the eruptions from Mauna Loa that bathed the sky in a red glow. Now she edges her way toward a blistering lava flow to explore it firsthand.

On this trek, Coloma wears long pants and a long-sleeved shirt made out of natural fibers. If the lava flow were larger, she would wear a heavy fireproof suit reinforced with metal to reflect the intense heat away from her body. With her hands protected by gloves, she takes the temperature of the lava using an electric thermometer made of steel, called a **thermo-couple**. A regular glass thermometer would melt in the 2100° F (1150° C) heat.

Since its most recent eruption began in 1983, Kilauea has been continuously spurting lava. So far, the flows from Hawaii's youngest volcano have covered more than 40 square miles (100 square km), adding nearly 600 acres of land to the Big Island. The flows have steamrolled through rainforests, historical sights, highways, and homes, causing more than $60 million in damages.

Near Kilauea's Pu'uO'o vent, Coloma prepares to take a sample from a **skylight**, an opening at the top of a pahoehoe lava tube. If Coloma isn't careful, the rock around the skylight could give way, sending her toppling down into tube. She

Volcanologists look into an active lava tube on Kilauea. Francine Coloma is closest to the camera.

tosses a sledgehammer attached to a long cable into the sky-light. When she pulls it back out, the hammer's head is coated with sizzling, orange lava. Coloma quickly drops the hammer into a bucket of cold water. She removes the hardened pieces of lava from the hammer and lets them cool a little longer in the water. Coloma wraps the chunks of lava in cloth bags for the trip home. Later, the samples will be sent out to a lab for

A Close Call

Coloma has never been seriously injured in the field, but once, while taking a sample of pahoe-hoe lava, she forgot to put on her longed-sleeved shirt. "As I dipped my hammer in the lava, the air around me felt hotter than the inside of an oven," she recalls. "My arm holding the hammer was red, like having a bad sunburn, and all the hair on my arm had burned off!"

43

analysis so scientists can learn more about what kind of rock makes up the deepest part of Earth.

Volcano Watch

Although working in the field is an important part of volcanology, most of Coloma's time is spent taking measurements, collecting data from instruments, and interpreting the information on computer. Scientists rely on many tools to help them monitor a volcano. One of the biggest indicators of volcanic activity is ground movement. This is called **deformation** and is caused by magma and rock shifting under the ground.

Deformation is measured in several ways. **Electronic distance measurement (EDM)** uses laser beams, or rays of light, to detect rising magma that may cause a volcano to swell or bulge. **Tiltmeters** note changes in the shape of a volcano electronically by reading the tilt, or angle, of the land. **Seismometers** buried in the ground around a volcano detect earthquakes. **Strainmeters**, 10-foot (3-m) long, fluid-filled tubes, are also placed below ground. When rock moves, it squeezes the fluid from one chamber to another. Strainmeters are so sensitive they can even pick up tiny shifts in the crust caused by the gravitational pull of the Sun and the Moon.

For the bigger picture, scientists rely on the **global positioning system (GPS)**, a network of satellites orbiting Earth. GPS sends a series of signals to receivers strategically placed around a volcano, allowing geologists to monitor tiny changes

Above, Francine Coloma positions an electronic distance measurement unit, which will shoot a red laser beam across a crater on Kilauea to measure distance. Below, Coloma is setting up a global positioning satellite unit, which will be used to measure movements in Earth's crust.

Fatal Blows

In the past four hundred years, Earth's volcanic eruptions have killed about 300,000 people.

in ground movement. GPS surveys have shown that each year, the southeastern section of Kilauea volcano is slowly sliding about 3 inches (8 cm) to the southeast.

Why Do They Do It?

Some volcanologists hike up windy trails to bury seismometers near a volcano. Others crawl into rocky crevices to measure the flow of toxic gases. Some, like Fran Coloma, trek onto ever-shifting crust to scoop up glowing globs of lava. Over the years, many geologists have lost their lives studying and observing volcanoes. Yet they take these risks willingly, knowing that each discovery may help them better forecast eruptions and, ultimately, save lives.

In 1985, nearly 23,000 people died in Armero, Colombia, when the eruption of Nevado del Ruiz sent enormous lahars sweeping into the valleys below. At the time, there was no team of scientists that could be called in an emergency to assist with an awakening volcano—something that would have, no doubt, saved countless lives. After the tragedy in Colombia, the USGS and the U.S. Office of Foreign Disaster Assistance formed the **Volcano Disaster Assistance Program (VDAP)**.

Just six years later, on June 15, 1991, Mount Pinatubo in the Philippines erupted in what was to be the largest eruption of the twentieth century. The blast pumped 1.2 cubic miles (5 cubic km) of ash 20 miles (35 km) into the sky. Hot, pyroclastic flows swept outward from the summit for nearly 10 miles (16 km), completely destroying a U.S. Air Force base. About

A Career For You

Are you curious about rocks, lava, and volcanoes? If you are and you like math, computers, and being outdoors, you might have what it takes to become a volcanologist.

three hundred people died, but scientists estimate that many thousands would have been killed had the VDAP response team not been there to monitor the volcano and encourage the evacuation of eighty thousand people.

Today, more than 500 million people around the world live near volcanoes. Some farm the rich, fertile lands created by them, while other simply enjoy the view. But the increase in population around volcanoes is a major concern for volcanologists, whose goal it is to keep people out of harm's way. Although developing technology is giving geologists new insight into how volcanoes behave, these unyielding forces continue to keep them on their toes. Over the course of its life, which spans 100,000 to 1 million years or more, a volcano may go through numerous stages, changing behavior, form, and shape many times over. If there is one thing scientists can be certain of, it is that no two volcanoes or volcanic eruptions are quite the same. Perhaps it is this unpredictable, untamable nature that keeps them forever spellbound by Earth's beautiful and mighty volcanoes.

Francine Coloma and a colleague take a gas sampling on Kilauea.

Glossary

aa—a type of lava flow containing rough chunks of cinders

active volcano—a volcano that is either currently erupting or has erupted at least once within the last ten thousand years

ash—bits of volcanic rock, usually less than 0.08 inches (2 mm) wide

ash cloud—a cloud of volcanic ash and dust created by an eruption

avalanche—a large volume of snow, ice, mud, rock, and debris traveling at high speeds

black smokers—undersea volcanoes with tall, pillarlike vents that spew super-heated, mineral-rich seawater

blocks—solid rock fragments tossed out in a volcanic eruption, ranging from 3 inches (7 cm) to 30 feet (9 m) wide or more

caldera—a large basin formed at the summit of a volcano by the collapse of the volcanic cone into its magma chamber

cinders—rock fragments thrown from a volcano measuring up to 2 inches (5 cm) wide; also called "lapilli," an Italian word meaning "little stones"

cinder cone—a cone-shaped volcano, usually measuring less than 1,000 feet (300 meters), formed by the accumulation of erupted cinders

core—the central region of Earth that lies below the mantle

crust—the rocky outer layer of Earth's surface that is broken up into tectonic plates

deformation—how the ground around a volcano shifts or moves

dormant volcano—a volcano that has not erupted within the last ten thousand years, but is expected to erupt in the future

dust—the finest particles of volcanic rock that may float into the upper atmosphere, where they may remain for some time

electronic distance measurement (EDM)—a way of measuring the tilt or angle of the ground surrounding a volcano using laser beams

extinct volcano—a volcano that is not erupting and is believed to have completed its life cycle

feeder pipe—a rocky conduit beneath Earth's crust that transports magma from the magma chamber up into the volcano

fissure—a long crack in Earth's crust, above or below sea level, which may be several miles (km) in length

fissure volcano—a type of shield volcano in which magma erupts from a fissure, or crack, on the surface

flood basalt—a plateau formed by lava flows that have cooled into huge, wide, thin sheets that are not a typical, volcano-shaped landform

fumarole—a volcanic vent that erupts mainly steam and gases

geologist—a scientist who studies the origin, structure, and composition of Earth; a geologist who specializes in studying and monitoring volcanoes is called a **volcanologist**

geothermal energy—energy harnessed from the internal heat of Earth in volcanic areas that is used to generate electricity, or geothermal power

global positioning system (GPS)—A network of space satellites orbiting Earth that scientists use to measure the movements and eruptions of volcanoes

hot spot—a stationary heat source located in Earth's mantle from which magma travels upward through a plate to form volcanoes

lahar—a massive volcanic mudflow that may carry trees, rocks, and other debris

lava—magma, or melted rock, that has reached the surface of Earth

lava bomb—a partially melted glob of lava thrown out of a volcano during an eruption that is twisted and elongated into various shapes, and is often football-like in appearance

lava dome—a steep-sided, rounded dome formed by eruptions of thick lava cooling around a vent; often formed in the craters and calderas of stratovolcanoes

lava flow—liquid lava that is moving over the surface of Earth

magma—melted rock and dissolved gases within Earth's crust

magma chamber—an underground storage area in Earth's crust where magma collects

mantle—the largest layer of Earth's interior that lies between the core and the crust and makes up about 70 percent of the planet's mass

oceanic ridge—a volcanic chain formed along an underwater rift zone where tectonic plates are spreading apart

pahoehoe—a type of lava flow with a smooth or wrinkly surface, in which tunnels of lava may continue flowing beneath the hardened outer crust

Pele's hair—lava that is blown by the wind into long strands of glassy fibers; named for the Hawaiian goddess of volcanoes

Pele's tears—lava that cools into glassy beads

pillow lava—interconnected, sacklike blobs of lava that form underwater

pumice—lava that cools before gas bubbles can escape, creating a frothy rock that may float on water

pyroclastic material—volcanic materials spewed from a volcano into the surface of Earth by a pyroclastic flow or fall

pyroclastic fall—volcanic debris from an eruption that is thrown onto the air; also called tephra

pyroclastic flow—a fluid mass of hot, dry dust, ash, and larger volcanic debris caused by a flow of hot gases that may travel from a volcanic vent at a high speed

rift zone—an area where Earth's tectonic plates are separating

Ring of Fire—the region of extensive volcanic and earthquake activity ringing most of the Pacific Ocean, where several tectonic plates border one another

seamount—an individual mountain on the seafloor that is usually volcanic

seismometer—an instrument that detects earthquakes, or rock fracturing within the planet's crust

shield volcano—a massive, gently sloping volcano with a flattened dome built by flows of erupting lava

skylight—an opening in the top of a pahoehoe lava tube

strainmeter—a 10-foot (3-m) long, fluid-filled tube buried in the ground around a volcano that measures deformation, or ground movement

stratovolcano—a steep-sloped volcano built by alternating layers of lava flows and pyroclastic eruptions; also called a composite volcano

subduction zone—the area where two tectonic plates collide and one sinks, or subducts, beneath the other

tectonic plates—the segments of Earth's crust that support continents, islands, and oceans

tephra—particles of solid or partially melted rock, such as dust, ash, cinders, lava bombs, and blocks, thrown from a volcano as part of a pyroclastic fall

thermocouple—an electric thermometer made of steel used to measure the temperature of molten lava

tiltmeter—an electronic instrument used to measure changes in the angle, or tilt, of the ground around a volcano

trench—a long, narrow furrow in oceanic crust that forms along a subduction zone where one tectonic plate slides under another

vent—an opening on the surface of Earth through which gases, lava, and rock erupt

vog—a pollutant formed when sulfur dioxide gas released from volcanoes reacts with sunlight, oxygen, dust particles, and water vapor in the air to create hazy clouds and, sometimes, acid rain

Volcano Disaster Assistance Program (VDAP)—a U.S.-sponsored team of scientists that responds to impending volcanic crises around the world, assisting with volcano monitoring and public safety

Volcanic Explosivity Index (VEI)—a scale scientists use to rate volcanic eruptions from 0 to 8, where each ranking is based on the force of the explosion, the amount of debris released, the height of ash cloud, the type of eruption, and how long the eruption lasted

volcano—one or more openings in Earth's crust where magma, gases, and/or rock emerge

volcanology—the branch of geology devoted to the study of volcanoes

To Find Out More

Books

Downs, Sandra. *Earth's Fiery Fury*. Brookfield, CT: Twenty-First Century Books, 2000.

Duey, Kathleen and Mary Barnes. *Freaky Facts About Natural Disasters*. New York, NY: Aladdin Paperbacks, 2001.

Farndon, John. *Volcanoes*. New York, NY: Dorling Kindersley, 1998.

Nicolson, Cynthia Pratt. *Volcano!* Tonawanda, NY: Kids Can Press, 2002.

Simon, Seymour. *Volcanoes*. New York, NY: Morrow Children's Books, 1998.

Videos and CD ROMS

Billion Dollar Disasters, Discovery Channel Video, 2001.

Perilous Beauty: The Hidden Dangers of Mount Rainier, U.S. Geological Survey, 1996.

Understanding Volcanoes, Discovery Channel Video, 1997.

Volcanoes, CD ROM & Book, Princeton, NJ: Two-Can Publishing, 2000.

Organizations and Online Sites

David A. Johnston Cascades Volcano Observatory
U.S. Geological Survey
1300 S.E. Cardinal Court, Bldg. 10, Suite 100
Vancouver, WA 98683
(360) 993-8900
http://vulcan.wr.usgs.gov
At this site you can tour the volcanoes in the Cascade chain, explore their history, and get the latest updates on volcanic activity. See amazing before and after photos of Mount St. Helens and discover what is happening on the mountain today.

Volcano World
University of North Dakota

Grand Forks, ND 58202

http://volcano.und.nodak.edu

This educational site offers fascinating volcano facts as well as movie clips of lava flows and volcanic eruptions. Click on the "kids' door" to learn more about the legends that volcanoes have inspired, test your volcano knowledge, and take a virtual tour of volcanoes on Earth as well as those in space.

Hawaiian Volcano Observatory
U.S. Geological Survey
P.O. Box 51
1 Crater Rim Drive
Hawaii Volcanoes National Park, HI 96718

http://hvo.wr.usgs.gov

Discover the latest news on eruptions at Kilauea volcano and Mauna Loa. Find out more about lava flows, deadly gases, and other volcanic hazards.

Volcano Hazards Program
U.S. Geological Survey
345 Middlefield Road
Menlo Park, CA 94025

http://volcanoes.usgs.gov

Learn about the Volcano Disaster Assistance Program and how geologists prepare for and react to volcanic eruptions around the globe. This site also offers a photo glossary and links to other U.S. volcano observatories.

A Note on Sources

Though I have always loved the heavenly grace of the Cascade Mountains, it wasn't until Mount St. Helens erupted in 1980 that I began to truly understand how the calm allure of these majestic peaks masked a devastating reality. Experiencing such a rare and remarkable event sparked my desire to know more about volcanoes and their impact around the world.

In writing this book, I called on many sources within the United States Geological Survey, including the Volcano Hazards Program and USGS observatories in the Cascades, Hawaii, and Alaska. I also looked to educational institutions, such as the Smithsonian's Global Volcano Program, Michigan Technical University, and the University of North Dakota's Volcano World. Further, I read numerous books, such as *Volcano Cowboys* by Dick Thompson, *Mount St. Helens: The Eruption and Recovery of a Volcano* by Rob Carlson, and Ruth Kirk's *Sunrise to Paradise: The Story of Mount Rainier National Park*. I relied on news accounts, video documentaries, and CD-ROM titles for additional insight into the topic area.

I am grateful to Dr. Elizabeth Nesbitt, Curator of Invertebrate Paleontology at the Burke Museum of Natural History and Culture at the University of Washington, a dedicated educator who provided invaluable knowledge and guidance. Also, thanks to Lyn Topinka of the Cascades Volcano Observatory and Jan Takahashi of the Hawaiian Volcano Observatory for their expertise. Special thanks to Francine Coloma, who so graciously shared her life's passion and allowed me to come along for a few steps of her amazing journey.

I still love the mountains and still find the Cascades calming and captivating. But things are different now. For I have seen both sides of a volcano, the quiet magnificence and the deadly might. And anyone who has done that is forever changed.

—Trudi Strain Trueit

Index

Numbers in *italics* indicate illustrations.

About the Author

Trudi Strain Trueit grew up in the shadow of Mount Rainier in Washington state. She witnessed the power of a volcano firsthand during the May 18, 1980, eruption of Mount St. Helens and has visited many of the volcanoes in the Cascades chain, from Mount Garibaldi in British Columbia, Canada, to Mount Shasta in northern California.

A former television news reporter and weather forecaster for KREM TV in Spokane, Washington, Trueit is a freelance writer and journalist who has written many books for the Franklin Watts Library Series. Her titles include *Rocks, Gems, & Minerals*; *Fossils*; *Earthquakes*; *Clouds*; *Storm Chasers*; *The Water Cycle*; and *Rain, Hail, & Snow*. Trueit earned a B.A. in broadcast journalism from Pacific Lutheran University in Tacoma, Washington. She and her husband, Bill, make their home in Everett, Washington, in view of Mount Baker, a 10,778-foot (3,285-m) active volcano in the north Cascades that occasionally vents plumes of steam.